■ □ ■ □ ■

CHARON'S FERRY

■ □ ■ □ ■

GYULA ILLYÉS

CHARON'S FERRY

FIFTY POEMS

Translated from the Hungarian
and with an introduction by Bruce Berlind

NORTHWESTERN UNIVERSITY PRESS

EVANSTON, ILLINOIS

Northwestern University Press
Evanston, Illinois 60208-4210

Printed in the United States of America

ISBN 0-8101-1798-3 (CLOTH)
ISBN 0-8101-1799-1 (PAPER)

Library of Congress Cataloging-in-Publication Data

Illyés, Gyula, 1902–
    Charon's ferry : fifty poems / Gyula Illyés ; translated from the
Hungarian and with an introduction by Bruce Berlind.
        p. cm. — (Writings from an unbound Europe)
    ISBN 0-8101-1798-3 (alk. paper) — ISBN 0-8101-1799-1 (pbk. : alk. paper)
    I. Berlind, Bruce. II. Title. III. Series.
PH3241.I55A6 2000
894'.511132—dc21

                                                        00-010142

■ □ ■ □ ■

CONTENTS

II One Sentence on Tyranny

III Nothingness Is Nearing

■ □ ■ □ ■

TRANSLATOR'S ACKNOWLEDGMENTS

THANKS ARE DUE THE EDITORS OF THE FOLLOWING PUBLICA-
tions, where many of these poems first appeared: *Arion, Bit-
terroot, Blue Unicorn, Columbia: A Magazine of Poetry and
Prose, Connecticut Poetry Review, Hungarian PEN, Light, New
Letters, Osiris, PEN International, Poetry East, Prose Poem, Sig-
nal, Silverfish Review, Texas Review, Visions International,* and
Webster Review.

I owe very special thanks to Mária Kőrösy, who for nearly
two decades provided me with working roughs of Hungarian
texts. But Mrs. Kőrösy's contributions to Hungarian litera-
ture, and to translations of it into English, go well beyond her
work with me. Until her retirement as English secretary of the
Hungarian PEN Club in Budapest, Mrs. Kőrösy assisted many
American, Canadian, Irish, and English poets who learned to
value Hungarian poetry and chose to devote their talents to
translating it. Her consequent importance to Hungarian letters
has gone largely unsung. I sing it here, with heartfelt gratitude.

I must also acknowledge the Council for International Ex-
change of Scholars, the Board of Foreign Scholarships of the
United States Information Agency, and the Hungarian Min-
istry of Culture for a Fulbright Research Award that enabled
me to spend six months in Hungary in 1984, when I began
translating Illyés, and the general secretary and staff of the
Hungarian PEN Club, as it then was, my hosts during the
Fulbright period.

■ □ ■ □ ■

TRANSLATOR'S
INTRODUCTION

UNTIL HIS DEATH IN 1983, GYULA ILLYÉS WAS HUNGARY'S preeminent man of letters. He was poet, novelist, playwright, editor, translator, literary and cultural historian. His socio-autobiographical account of peasant life on a feudal estate, called *People of the Puszta,* would alone have assured his place in Hungarian letters. If pressed, some Hungarians would concede that one or two of his contemporaries had produced individual poems, even bodies of poetry, of higher quality; yet among those readers, few would have denied Illyés his position of preeminence—even as a poet. The apparent contradiction is partially explained by Illyés's personal characteristics and attainments. He was a *presence* in a sense few literary figures have enjoyed. (A Hungarian friend poses Dr. Johnson as analogue.) Though largely self-taught, his erudition was immense, and his intellectual honesty was such that his judgment in all matters almost always prevailed. The most frequent summation is that he was the "grand old man" of Hungarian letters. More than that, this presence, this grand old man, was the conscience of his people, and an understanding of that role requires some explanation of the tradition within which Illyés wrote and of the value placed upon that tradition by Hungarian readers and critics.

Illyés was a poet of the people in a sense unknown in the West. Insofar as the term, or something like it, has been applied in the United States, it has been used to sentimentalize popular, usually "anti-intellectual," writers with vague social sympathies and a prevailing optimism about America and about the essential goodness of the hardworking masses— Carl Sandburg comes readily to mind. In Hungary it is a serious critical category—the word "populist" appears most frequently—to designate a poet of peasant background who is perceived as embodying and expressing broadly cultural values that are still operative, or felt to be operative. He is, in this sense, a national poet, one whose private concerns are inextricable from the history and aspirations of his country. It is an ancient position and an ancient tradition, which, however, began in earnest in the mid–nineteenth century, when the prototypical ideal was established by Sándor Petőfi, generally regarded as Hungary's greatest poet, who joined, and gave his life for, the ill-fated revolution of 1848. It is more than coincidence that the standard biography of Petőfi was written in the 1930s by Gyula Illyés.

Illyés was the conscious inheritor of the Petőfi tradition. It's not that his poems are chauvinistic or even overtly celebratory (in the manner, say, of Whitman) of national ideals. It's that they are rooted in cultural values, incorporate cultural motifs, and have behind them the weight of Hungarian history, particularly its history of suppressions and survivals. The result is *lyric,* ostensibly *personal,* poetry which, however, resonates—more often than not faintly—in a political way. The poem "Crows," to cite one instance, is political in just that sense. To be sure, there are others of Illyés's poems that are political in more obvious ways; the most famous example is "One Sentence on Tyranny," a poem of 1950 whose reputation was chiefly underground until 1986, when it was published in a book for the first time. But for the most part, the political import of Illyés's poetry is more subtle, more pervasive, less prompted by local and occasional events. His return to Hungary after a five-year exile in Paris following the abortive revolution of 1919—a return that was clearly the conscious assumption of Petőfi's mantle—inaugurated his mission as spokesman and defender of the people's rights; and many of the poems concerned with social justice, repression, and tyranny, which he wrote from time to time throughout the remainder of his life, declare their stances more explicitly. Still, it does Illyés a disservice to view them as the center of his oeuvre. Notwithstanding the popularity (and indeed stature) of many of those poems, by far the great bulk of his poetry is lyric.

The years in Paris were important, partly in a negative sense. While it's true that he studied psychology and French literature at the Sorbonne, and that he consorted with many of the principal surrealists of his generation—Aragon, Breton, Cocteau, Éluard, Tzara (see "Two Flashes into the Past")—it is also true that his return to Hungary must be seen as a rejection of one set of literary values in the interests of another, a choice substantiated by the virtual expunging, in his poetry, of the surreal techniques he had begun to master and the espousing of a more realistic style.*

It was already a vanished world that Illyés evoked, as many poems make clear. (See especially "Ebb Tide," "World Collapse," and the second section of "Two Flashes into the Past," but many others touch on this awareness in one way or

---

* The significance of Illyés's Parisian sojourn is still more complex, as is clear from these remarks made during a television interview the year before he died: "I must confess that the reason I am grateful for my five years in Paris is that when I returned I was able to discover the world. I could have gone back to Paris—there was the opportunity—but it was my Parisian mind which made me grasp that this is my *material,* that this place is mine, that this is where I must be doing something. . . . If I had not been in Paris, I would never have understood this" (*New Hungarian Quarterly* 34 [autumn 1983]: 23–24). It is also true that from time to time—especially in his prose poems—he reverted to surrealistic techniques, as, for example, in "Successful Effort," which is about his return from the French experience.

another.) There is something anachronistic about the notion of a peasant tradition in a society that is increasingly industrialized; and as economic and educational conditions in the provinces improve, as agriculture becomes more and more mechanized, and—perhaps most important—as television becomes more and more accessible, the very fact of a peasant society, as distinct from a merely agrarian one, will cease to exist. And so it is less and less likely that a public poet of Illyés's stature will rise again. It is difficult today to find a poet under the age of sixty whose sense of identity incorporates the values and attitudes that made possible a Petőfi or an Illyés.

And it would seem too that Illyés himself apparently became disillusioned with the role. The selection that follows is in three parts, the first two comprised of poems written over a span of nearly half a century, the third of late poems that were published posthumously. What is remarkable about the later poems is not merely their obsession with death, which had been prominent in Illyés's poetry almost from the beginning, but also their private, almost hermetic, sense of helplessness. It's as if, with death around the next corner, he could no longer feel sustained by a sense of solidarity—as if he felt the whole course of public events to be happening outside himself, and as if he had decided to indulge his darkest vision, a vision that hardly accords with the Illyés the old establishment could extol as a public figure. The old Illyés is not completely absent—"Phoenix," for example, is a deeply political poem—but more often than not, one has the sense of an old man meditating, in isolation, at times bitterly, on the *in*efficacy of the human will as it confronts the shambles of civilization.

There is a classical purity to Illyés's language, a formal, even stately, quality of restraint, which may strike some modern American ears as a bit arch, possibly archaic. I considered eliminating it in my translations but decided that it was too central a component of his tone to be ignored without serious distortion—without, that is, mistranslating an essential element of his work. And I realized, as well, that it was precisely the tone that Illyés's subject matter required. Among the priorities that my response to him established as guidelines for my work as translator, preserving (or translating) that tone remained high.

■ □ ■ □ ■

CHARON'S FERRY

I

. . . Rocking . . .

Flood

The gardens are afloat in water, the small village
a peninsula now. And the deluge increases.
We've done what it's possible for man to do.
It's black as pitch outside, not a star shines through.
Whatever's to be done must be left to God to do.

In a stinking oil lamp's smog in the old schoolroom
the congregation sings the Anthem, then
the Psalm, then finally "In Thy will
we trusted! . . ." Caps and hats in hand;
the veins in necks and bald heads swell,
forelocks and ducktails flap in their zeal.
Abruptly a young girl's bell-tongued voice
breaks out of the gloom like a knell.

And the vicar sings, and the priest sings,
and the priest's gaunt wife with her ten children,
and soot and the stench of thick boots rise
and the yellow tongue of the lamp falters
and the whole world has become an ocean,
and fiercer and fiercer with every minute the skies
pour down their winter rain on the dark waters.

Bodroghalász, January 24, 1948

Hope in the Air

The swallows, the storks, have returned;
and circling, seeking their vanished nests,
for fleeting seconds erect and reerect
the church tower toppled to the ground.

And the rectory's chimney too
(on Christmas Eve
the bombs hurled it—to the earth?—a heave
straight into the blue!)

What delicate airy stuff it's made of,
that tower
built by the swallows' love!

Nor for an hour
will I forget the chimney
built anew by two storks' memory!

The Last Home

I'd like to return home at night
to a small village in the Pyrenees,
so many saints and x's in its long name,
they don't deliver the mail higher than that;
only the alpine sheep of the stars, maybe,
wander higher. "Who is it?"
My mother opens the door, my grandmother,
they hug me, question me (in Catalan,
of course, or in Basque, and that's the way
I answer): the journey was exhausting but
there's no other news, I'm fine,
glad to be here for homemade food and wine;
and at last—in my old place once again—
sleep a great dream of oblivion.

Charon's Ferry

Charon's ferry does not depart with us when
    our eyes have closed and iced over.
Mournful crossers, it's for long and with eyes wide open
    we move on the fateful water.

Our jealous destiny drives us, years before,
    into the boat; and we rock with it.
It glides—though not to our liking—along a shore
    equally exquisite;

equally beautiful as on lagoons or *canali,*
    those of honeymooners.
Surely it's all the same: sky, journey, scenery
    —only in reverse!

Everything's equally exquisite, in fact—mystically—
    as it fleets away, more exquisite even!
Something like what happens to a melody
    when it leaves the violin.

Laughing, we sit among friends and trees
    —cheerful gibes go round—
and all of a sudden the ferry begins to rock with us
    (just us!), outward bound.

He's wise who smiles at this pleasure cruise.
    When he weeps, his tears should then
be in thanks for so many piazzas, such Casa d'Oros,
    though he won't see them again.

In a Blacksmith's House
on the Puszta

I look out.
    Everything's milkwhite.
Icicles hang from the eaves like
so many sharp-pointed sharks' teeth.
    Winter
    ate me.

I am Jonah.
    But instead of
the whale this monster drifts with me,
he alone knows to what Pontus.
    And I'm
    godless.

No one awaits me,
    pursues me.
This little room is a fish gut.
It's warm, so I don't mind the fumes
    of lard,
    the stench.

One such bore me.
    One such rocked me,
childhood, under your deep water.
I entrust myself to it once
    again.
    I'm home.

The storm—time too—
    tosses me up
and down, confronts me constantly.
And yet—just by assaulting me—
    drifts me
    onward.

We may reach
    some degree of spring.
Meanwhile, we can afford to sing
until this monster of a fish
    vomits
    us up.

Bacon, cabbage,
    onions, salt, bread
for weeks will lie on the table.
And thus I hear how I travel,
    brought by
    winter!

White

On the snow-blown ground
tiny, silent wind flurries—
   White
   mice—
one surfaces, cautiously,
stirs, scurries,
a moment.

Promptly hurries down—
   why?
   Hi!
To break out again.

   All ears, scampers
here! there! See, under the trees!

Whiter than white.

How much more real is
silence, when it lives.

Look—on the snow,
the wind motion—it grimaces.
   Makes faces.

The sun is shining.

The snow is shining.

The sky today is brand-new too.

From a treetop a pinch of snow
rustles off, like lightning.

What a hullabaloo.

That was the final effort.

Oh world of fulfillment,
   future, future.

When everything will be over.

Photograph

Don't enlarge this one, but . . . where's that alpine one
    . . . the one that shows . . .
Here it is! . . . that shows me swept by my skis
    clear over the bushes!

Did I take a spill? Later! But here in this one I'm still
    —look—in flight!
Frame this one, you can look at it over my head
    whenever you like;

this one, when I'm old and crumple to sleep by the fire,
    stiff and numb,
—the curve of a seagull, my essence!—please
    rescue this one.

See this one in my place when you stare at my chair,
    empty one day.
This is what loved you, this is what swept—forever—
    you too away.

Crows

Crows sit perched on the bare birch boughs
and the snowstorm's surging billows
with indrawn necks (I watch them from
my upstairs bedroom window),
and thus they row, in rhythm they go
in the longer- and longer-whistling blow,
black as pitch in the pure white snow
(why everyone bullies them off but I)
in this giant winter grown to the sky
—thus back and forth, leaning together,
they hurtle against the howling weather,

almost asleep in their blind flight
onward to the future, trusting their fate
to the task of their talons, stubborn as steel
—perching thus they journey on,
more sure they'll arrive than any traveler,
        than any sailor, can feel.

        They bring me good news of spring
            in this language more silver-tongued
than the lily of the valley, the dew, the dove—

        The most loyal allies of the Sun—

Bearing in their tiny heartbeats' tropics
the ancient faith of the great will—of
what triumphed over glacial epochs.

Evening Song

I have brought home

                    The hunter his quarry
                    The teamster his load
                    The reaper his fatigue

   This day too

The window light that at night keeps watch:
                             the Good
                             in the Evil

   The house:
                where someone expects me

   This is my place

Yet my wages—a mouthful of death

Existence has grown godless, not the heart

   Sleep with me

The Found Caravan Diary

Only the compass now hoped,
stammered: spoke,
with its palsied tongue, a sign: somewhere
is something can answer.

We kept at it;
again a dayful of desert.

A rocky wall,
a cuneiform scrawl.

Line upon line, confused, dogged:
wrinkles on a mad forehead.

Here, the stuck
struggle of old Time.

Dumbstruck.

As only the wind shrieks.

Sand on the eyelid. Sand between sweaty toes.
Sand, when the jaws close.

We killed our road-wise camel.
Had a final meal.

Termites

My body, what I am in fact,
my inner self, the essence, has no mind
to see the world; it assigned
two shortsighted sentries for that.

When I'm wounded, it spurts blood,
mixes mortar, quickly plasters over
the part where danger could bother
the subcutaneous abode.

Our billions of inherited cells
were perhaps the people of an open city
fluttering about indefinitely.

But having experienced Evil, they then
locked themselves up in their termite castle.
Now even I don't know who they might have been.

The Salvation of the Damned

Happiness has happened. Yes, this. We may marvel at it.
And light a cigarette.

We have become mortal again.
We may exchange our observations,
our policies pro tem

on this and that, and also on "we shall die!"
on what the future hides, namely.

The still cannibal
heart is . . . well, well . . . gentle—
spies out from its beast's den.

So we may even get to know each other a little,

as long as some residual
substance from Eden's primeval factory
continues to function quietly
in the sinless recesses of our bodies.

As long as the hormones fabricate
a little of that divine proclivity

for letting our bodies devour each other,
we may ascend to heaven for another moment.

The Year Drops Anchor, Tihany

The sunflowers bend their heads to the ground,
a crowd of condemned convicts.
In the village they're sharpening sickles
to cut their throats, like hatchets.

Willow leaves flutter sideways over the lake
like a young girl's yellow locks.
Here and there the wind grates on the water.
Swallows gather in flocks.

The boat, like a lazy ox now, all morning
jangled its rusty chain,
jangled so hard you thought it would bolt,
come loose, rear up, break rein.

But it's quiet now. Who made the potatoes?
Conceived, bore them? In summer brightness
they dry themselves on their mother earth's
warm belly and breasts.

There's no path in the vineyard, only
trails of the rake. It's nearly harvesttime.
Their long black-and-white goat udders
hang from the heavy vines.

The silent lake guards the peace of its surface
—its grandeur so reassuring—
guards the fisherman, the hill, the boat,
and gratefully doubles everything.

Golden days. No longer need to work.
Time just dawdles. And now the ferry's here,
noiselessly running, its engines all but stopped,
heaped with its cargo, the Year.

Grip

Every root
in the long run
a fist.
While a molecule lives
the tree sticks to its guns,
fights with a grip.

It answers
there
the wind's invective.

Ebb Tide

In the marketplace, no children.
In the side streets, the aged. . . .

The whole village,
like a blimp, has been airborne.

Ten meters above the ground
incorporeally hover
the school, the parish house,
the old bullock-browed church.

The meat market flew off a year ago.
The veterinarian's home is also airborne.

The cemetery, grappling with infinity,
eating the shoreline from time out of mind,
silently marches off
with its ever scarcer furrows of surf
lit by the moon, leaving behind
a hodgepodge
of bones and barge wreckage.

Successful Effort

The ship went down, with a big bump reached the bottom of the sea, and keeled over. It now turns out that it was a country, a nation. "After a hurricane." I was a passenger, but somehow or other—due to sheer chance or because, in spite of the storm, I'd gone up on deck to look around—a current (I held on to the railing in vain) carried me up to the surface. The sun was shining. Yachts were racing on the calmed water. My friends, flying along in a boat, cried out in a foreign language, but so clearly, in words as cleanly luminous as the sparkles of sun on the rippling water. Of the shipwreck—or even of the storm—they knew nothing. I laughed, I drank—the ambrosial Banyuls. And because—again by sheer chance—I knew how to handle the sails, I could become, then and there, a happy member of the *équipage*. Together we took possession of the wreath of victory.

It took me five years and a thousand tricks to get back to the ship on the bottom of the sea, where whoever hadn't perished had gone mad.

World Collapse

It's not my own death
        I regret, but
the house at Egres, that with me
        sinks in the dust.

In the dust for good, because
        it no longer exists.
It was pulled down twenty years ago
        for its prewar bricks.

The attic falls in,
        the dovecote
(my brother's) inside it.
    Everything comes to nothing.
        Falls to pieces, flies every which way.

There Will Be No War

N.N. was startled from his dawn slumber by the fuzzy image of a gigantic gorilla approaching his bed. But then the animal's ridiculously large stature (roughly two and a half meters), its six enormous fangs, its sneer beyond all animal as well as human scale, along with its murderous passion, were so dreamlike that N.N. settled down, shut his eyes, and laid his head back on the pillow. His faith in the world being unshakable. In the morning—next day? next decade?—the Sun lit upon him ripped to bloody shreds.

II

One Sentence on Tyranny

One Sentence on Tyranny

Where there's tyranny
there is tyranny,
not just in gun barrels,
not just in jails,

interrogation cells,
the sentry's calls
challenging the night,
there is tyranny not

just in the smoke-dark burnt
flaming prosecutor's indictment,
not just in confessions,
in Morse wall taps in prisons,

"One Sentence on Tyranny" has a somewhat complicated history of publication. What is certain is that it was not Illyés's response to the events of 1956, although the authorities believed it to be so for many years after. It was almost certainly written in 1950, one of the worst of the Stalinist years, when it could not of course have been published. It was, however, published during that small window of possibility at the height of the revolution ("counterrevolution," as the regime called it) on November 2, 1956—two days, that is, before Soviet tanks crushed the uprising—in a Budapest journal called *Irodalmi újság* (*Literary Gazette*). But the publication was hasty, and Illyés, having agreed to permit the poem to be included, had no time to find a manuscript and wrote it down from memory, omitting thereby seventeen lines that were subsequently restored. The two-hundred-line version appeared in a Zagreb journal in 1971, but it was not until 1987 that the poem appeared again in Hungary, and not until the following year—five years, that is, after Illyés's death—that it was included for the first time in one of his books. I have chosen to use the shorter, originally published, version, since it was the one that Hungarians knew as a silent rallying cry for three decades.—TRANSLATOR

not only in the chilly
verdict: the judge's "guilty,"
there is tyranny
not only in the soldierly,

crackling, "ten-hut!"
in "fire!" in the drumbeat,
in the way that
they drag corpses to the pit,

not only in the news
in fearful whispers
passed through furtively
half-opened doors, not only

in the hushing finger
dropped on the mouth,
there's tyranny not only
in the sturdy

bar-solid faces, the
wordless shrieks of woe
struggling in those bars,
in the mute tears'

torrents magnifying
the silence,
in the glassy pupils,

there's tyranny not just in
the standing ovation
of roared hurrahs,
of songs and cheers,

where there's tyranny
there is tyranny
not just in the unremitting
booms of palms applauding,

in the trumpet, the opera house,
the lying, strident, sonorous
stones of statues,
in colors, galleries of pictures,

in each separate frame,
it's in the brush and paint,
not only in the soft glide
of car noises at night

and the way
it stops at the door;

where there's tyranny
it's everywhere,
in everything as
not even your old god was;

there's tyranny in
the kindergartens,
in the fatherly counsel,
the mother's smile,

in the way the child
answers a stranger;

not only in barbed wire,
in book phrases more
deadly stupid-making
than barbed wire; it's there

in the good-bye kiss
as the wife says
when will you be home dear,
it's there

in the street, the customary
how-are-you's, the abruptly
softer grip, the slack
of the handshake,

there as your lover's face
turns suddenly to ice,
because it's with you
in the rendezvous,

not just the interrogation,
it's in the declaration,
in the rapturous moan,
like the fly in the wine,

because even in your dreams
you're not alone; it's even
in the marriage bed, and earlier
in the desire,

because what you think lovely
he's had already; it's he
who lay with you in bed
when you thought you loved,

on the plate, in the glass,
the mouth, the nose,
in cold, in twilight,
indoors and out,

as if the window were open
and a dead-flesh stink blew in,
as if somewhere gas
were escaping into the house;

if you talk to yourself it's he
who puts the question to you,
you're not free even
in your own imagination,

and the Milky Way: a zone
where border searchlights pan,
a whole field full of mines;
every star a spy hole,

the teeming celestial tent:
a single labor camp;
because tyranny speaks
from fever, the torture rack,

the priest who hears your confession,
the ringing of bells, the sermon,
from parliament, from church:
all those theatrical stages;

you shut your lashes, open them,
you're under observation;
like illness, like memory,
it keeps you company;

the rumbling train wheels whisper
a prisoner, you're a prisoner,
beside the sea, on the mountain,
it's this that you breathe in;

lightning flashes, it's there
in each unexpected murmur,
it's there in the light,
the jolt of the heart;

in tranquillity, in this
shackled tediousness,
in the pelting downpour,
these sky-high bars,

the incarcerating snowfall
white as a cell wall,
that eyes you through the eyes
of your dog, and because

it's in all you aspire to,
it's in your tomorrow,
in all that you think,
every move you make,

as a riverbed is cut,
you follow it, create it;
it's you who spies from this circle?
he's in the mirror, watchful,

he sees you, escape's absurd,
you're the prisoner, also the guard;
it seeps into the fabrics
of your clothes, your tobacco's

aroma, it eats into
your marrow bones; you'd
have ideas, but those
that come to you are his,

you'd look, but what you see
he's conjured up for you,
and a forest fire, lit
since you didn't stomp it out

when you tossed a match to the ground,
flames up now all around;
so his eyes are on you, sleepless,
in factory, field, and house,

and you don't feel anymore
what even bread and meat are,
what it is to desire, to love,
to open your arms, to live,

so the servant himself forges
and wears his own manacles;
if you eat, you're feeding him;
it's for him you beget children;

where there's tyranny everyone
is a link in the same chain;
it flows and festers from you,
you yourself are tyranny;

like moles in the sun, we walk
blind in the pitch-dark,
as restless in the closet
as we are in a desert;

because where there's tyranny
everything's vanity,
song, like this one faithful,
any art at all,

because from the beginning
he's been standing at your grave,
it's he who says who you've been,
even your dust serves him.

III

Nothingness Is Nearing

Consternation

Maggot-twitching vein, and tendon—
What's happened? It rivets my gaze—:
I would pluck back my hand
from the flash fire of my days!

Postcard from the Provinces

To take up arms—against leaf mold!—
grim Moses horns on the forehead?
To dig up the putrid foliage
to learn what the vile fates wanted?

And why has no dawn brought us
eyes that are less benighted?
No, I don't run with an army
where only wrath is foresighted.

On the World of Faith

Since we began putting our dead into the depths of the earth, we may have become convinced that the whole path of our life leads downward. There were people who consigned their departed to decay on the tops of trees, cliffs, and towers made expressly for that purpose: instead of worms, birds. Had we adopted that practice, I feel, our way of looking at the world and at life would be more casual, our temperament more cheerful. Perhaps it's not too late. Let's try all the paths. Toward transcendence, over there, toward the upper empyreans? With the Compass of Beliefs and Religions? If the crematoria chimneys and their playful smoke—playful even in that role—did not disfigure one of the most horrible falls of man, the brain could grope in that direction too.

A Nest for Seasons in the Concrete Jungle

I've looked for years at the tiny garden
    outside my room.
    It's a nest: for seasons
blundering into forests of stone.

Green spring, russet summer, yellow fall, white winter,
    so—in this dim cell—
    drag on. Live!—:
after a fashion,—as they've got accustomed.

One by one they come. Get by on little,
    these wild-winged ones of outer space:
    frugally, in exile, stay on.
    Yet the old eye unwearied still,
        awaiting them.

Procession in the Fog

Wind blows. A drunken reeling
village wedding procession;
but then I've also seen
   —and remember still—
a crowd of tippling mourners:
so those two rows of poplars,
   as down from the hill
     in autumn
    they stride in the fog,
    arm in arm supporting
    each other, from time
    to time merrily
glancing backward, seeming to
beckon you, you, why are you
loafing, the procession's been waiting
for a long time, are you coming?

Phoenix

1

Journey into the past (Pannonia)

Down on the Sió plain the faithful churches
    are ruins of pyramids and sphinxes
in the milkwhite of the moon. The blind clocks
    on the brows of their towers (for how long
        handless?) conform
to astrology according to Chaldaeus.

What's the hurry when there's no progress?

The childhood train rattles,
with its jolting wheels counts off
    timeless minutes to my soles.

    I'm free!—Free for where?

Ahead of us, up on the old feeder,
    on the low, steep
    curves of knolls, the track
    twists like a noose,
    tightens the loop.
It scares me that it leads back,
    there, to repeat—
where people can only be slaves—

Back to our yesterday? To our stone age?

2

Still, onward

The telephone poles downhill
    thicken to a picket fence.
        All speeds intoxicate.
Uphill, like an accordion,
    the poles separate.

    Whenever he hears them,
    snatches of music take
    the traveler by his arm:
old litanies? prayers at wakes?

3

And onward still

On the plains of Somogy not black but white
    was the color of women's mourning weeds
    in our great-grandmothers' time.
We could manufacture—the raw material's here—
    a regional mythology designed
    to conform to our own needs:
a message sent across thousands of years
    by the deep conscious from the deep past—
        Although
        Yes, although . . .

    The inferno-journey—
precisely the vision that must not lie!

4

More persistently

Sedulously the moonlight limes
    to death's pale hue
only the loftier, the statelier walls.
    Where the darkness falls
death whitens from oblivion.
    Secret signs
are sent by the distance. Would
    some sort of purity
    from the purgatory
of another censorious world
      be understood?

Has the future, as well, fallen
in the lightening sea of the past?

Will youth be a phoenix at last?

So much much weight falls from my heart,
    I am lightened. I am relieved,
in an earthly eternal element, I could say—
    in a flood of flame, maybe?

What's behind me is now before me.

The train lugs me, bumps on with a hobble,
I shuffle along in the dust, a slug, miserable—

But a bird flutters above me, stricken,
  its wings broken. Struggling,
  it frees itself. Again, again . . .

Christian Humanity

1

Each time (child of the puszta) I closed
    the blade of the jackknife,
I renewed my manhood. I could as well
    be a taker of life.

2

Because it limped, we drove the little calf
    to the marketplace.
We left it there. I—not looking back—
    my humanity, a piece.

World Order

I gave up on the world of stars.
Why? It's order! Order! Slavish order!
    Distance makes it more stifling still.
    A jail finally, if you see it clearly.
What free chaos a single cell
    of your brain unlocks! What infinity
    it creates from a spark of desire!
    What God makes is reality.

A place he carpenters for our soul to dwell.

You Could Have Spotted Me

You could have spotted me, Almighty One,
because—if indeed it's true
you exist and see (like the Eye in the old icon)—
because I haven't knocked, haven't disturbed you,

haven't wiggled my wounds toward you, or,
as you see, my worth: so I've followed your lead!
My mother taught me decorum—I didn't implore—
and my father stiff-necked pride—I didn't wheedle—

and to tell the truth, it's precisely Faith
—your faith?—taught me that here on this earth,
exile in myself as I am, with or against you,

something can be accomplished by a man like me.
I've not been an easy son to you. So,
consider me when there's a vacancy in the army.

With a Stranger

For a quarter of an hour decrepitude flowed
into all my limbs. Then drained out slowly.
What was it? I lie here sickened. Lewd
fornication it was. How much I'd enjoy
    kicking out all the strangers. For good.

Scene from a Drama

Fear of death? I know. It has arrived.
I deplore now squandering a single day
for nothing—a single minute! I hoard them
with a miser's tightness, I guard them,
let them trickle through my fingers, alone.
Why? I don't know. But I feel that whoever
breaks in on me to loot my golden solitude
is the thief of my treasures, literally
a housebreaker . . . Write letters, essays,
send a collection of poems—

                 . . . Here they lie,
a full shelf of the choice ones;
I wipe away cobwebs from
this or that bottle, sniffing and
shoving away the musty ones, the acidic,
those smelling of wood or cork or mice,
and all that are watered—a taste at last,
as the host rolls it on his tongue,
testing whether it's ropy, sedimented,
offensive, if its alcohol content is right,
and only then pours, first into his own glass
—holding it to the light to see if it's grainy—
then into his friends', one after the other,
nodding silently that now it can be lifted,
throat set, eyes shut,
he sends forth his thanks—like a smoke offering to heaven.

I rejoice that at least at this you're competent.

The Final Journey of the Leaves

The final journey of the leaves! Not
that scarcely audible, soft circling-down
from the skyward branches to the ground.
Not that virginal fall! But
the scurry down below, the whirling
from under shrubbery, beside hedgerows,
into the mud-filled puddles, then in time
to the sodden fields. Disorder, grime!
It's not the autumn winds that drive
the death march of these dead hands, these rattling
palms, but—do you feel it?—the winds of spring!
The young wife sweeps the litter away.
Why, for a second even, would she raise
    her hand in protest—
    she'd better drop it:
    time runs out,
    the old man bows his head.

Under the Ice-Bright Moon

All the sentry boxes in place.
Wooden kiosks at the barracks corners.
The castle rampart for walking guard with bayonet.
A wooden tower for ambushing—not game—men.
One-man stone niches for spying;
notches to shoot from. Isolated concrete
bunkers. All of them exist,
empty under the ice-bright moon.
But the discrepancy between awareness of danger
and acquiescence in it has thus far stretched
the ears taut. The sacred cause is gone, but
avoidability and inevitability
don't want to mix. When every rustle
—in the sties too—dies down, the noise of battle
has all the earmarks (fearmarks) of coming not
from behind the hill but from among the stars.

To Those Who Dread War

What is the one
medication for death?
The human intellect long ago hit on it!
The danger is purely imaginary.
Because if It, the Monster, got here,
however horribly,
It would mow down our empty place,
not us.
Because it's us or It. Because each
excludes the other in time and space:
thus preached
the highest Lord, the ancient logician,
the order of the Beginning and the End.
And today the new God-brained
Science may preach the dispersal of gloom:
how could war break in on
us—perceptibly?
The moment it entered our planet-home,
simultaneously
we'd be gone
—*à Dieux!*

Two Flashes into the Past

1. Rue Bonaparte

I peeped in, but still did not enter
the tiny bookshop.
Adrienne Monnier's. There at noon were huddled
the giant generation of my time:
Larbaud, MacLeish, Hemingway, Paulhan, Breton,
disputing if our culture will continue to live,
or if dust and ruin will settle on it for good
—the damage of Gide's and Nietzsche's assault on God.
I stepped in. To this day
I cannot know the fate of our human race.
The lively Adrienne waited on me at once.
I stole away, mortal,
well mannered, unredeemed.

2. Taking Notes on the Rostrum

The Calvinist girls! The rich! Only-children from
the right side of town, who at high festivals still
sported their great-grandmothers' leather waistcoats,
    assembling in their churchyard,
then filing in to their separate places
    with downcast eyelashes,
    so the only protest
    to the young boys' ogling
    was the ancient language
    of their decorous tread.

Sarahs, Rebeccas, Esthers,
what journey led your old—beautiful—eyes
    to question so candidly
    my loyal eyes, that maybe
    they too blink a bit ironically
       at this
meeting of a writer and his readers organized
by the home—your home—for aged cooperative members?

Thus you fly, buzzing my hand on the table,
    but arcing up and away
    whenever I'm sure that now
    I will catch you, history, on the wing.

Transformed Regions

1

The scenery changed, but at once,
　　when van Gogh came.
　　He flung his glance at it:
he fixed his horror on it!
　　Effectual curse—:
his sick spirit broods here
　　over the Waters—

2

You most ruthless of wizards, Picasso,
　　because an oracle too.
"The world is insane, insane!"
　　But judgment is imminent:
the enraged confrontations scream
　　each other down, those
psychic images—surer than photographs—
　　that forecast the future.

Unsteadily

If your feet slip stepping in mud,
    give them a wider spread
like the double legs of a capital *A*—
    but the lie of your forehead
    should be upward, anyway!

The Persecuted

No streetlights. From a row of blind buildings
through a suddenly opened door, the light,
with a pointed dagger's
rage, stabs at you.

Also from there, the Morse code blips
of a light-signal's speech: there's—where?—humanity!

Because of an ambush-issued noise,
startled,
gamelike, you cock your ears.
The old landscape is a wolf's den.

Trembling, you steal yourself
through this doubly soundless night—

What waits?

To the blind the world is narrow.
And wide as the firmament.

According to whether they know who you are.

And how the indictment varies.

Heart-boggling, how relief
presents itself:
chain-breaking escape artist, you may throw off
all the fetters of honor.

From a Philosopher's Insights

1

No, it's not the roof-shaking storm
    you must listen for;
    meanwhile you hear
that soft stammer which with a gnat's
vocabulary was
—no, not recited—merely buzzed,
by the *anima mundi,* in any willing ear.

2

The faucet's flawless drop elongates.
    Looks for a shape. Apple? Pear?
Opts for the pear, the sucker,
and drops off, fulfilling its fate,
    into the cloaca.

Nothingness Is Nearing

In the Sunday afternoon
so-to-speak breezeless village silence:
a repeated succession of bangs.
Still, not, after all, of guns.

They're playing skittles in Schmidek's inn.
From sixty years back. This thus old familiar—that is,
the noise appeasing the subconscious—
is more familiar still when it cuts out:
now, and there too, the two competing teams are drinking
                beer together
from the kitty collected in the tin plate.

The timeless frame of silence
grows prodigally pitted with human rustling,
in every village, obviously everywhere. "Short-supply item":
the awkward phrase's analogue, "short supply of noise,"
can be bracingly assimilated by the conscious.

The continually receding tiny rustlings
gradually saturate it, so that—gradually empty
earth and sky to such a degree of noiselessness,
that—take a breath!—
Nothingness is the nearest.

On a Private Golgotha

Now my shadow alone
is crucified from behind
and cast ahead by the sun.
I stalk it without success.
    The light is merciless:
    you're not the only one.

Hearty Welcome

A shy visit of
    untouched young girls
is this unexpected, feathery snowfall.
    Seasons, too, have their virginity.

Enough if nodding my head I reciprocate
the tribute outside my house
    from my wood-heated room.

I have crackers in an unopened box,
sweet liqueur in a bottle,
    appropriate words in my head,
readiness of limb to open the door—

Or in my eyes—thus, through the window—
a welcoming look, nevertheless,
    from a farther region, a remoter one,
and also the jingle of sleigh bells in the ear.

Let's place right there, in front of the stairway,
    the willow basket of gifts
      with the obvious bonus of my years.

In the Armchair of Creaking Bones

Shoo, shoo: how nimbly!—now not days
(in cotillion, like ballet girls fleet as air)
the weeks whisk by, the autumns, springs!
They've swung me around, and now—I only stare:

another decade gone—and yet another!
    Some of them pirouetting
back, as away they flutter
      beyond the wings.

They're well trained, as good pupils are.
Don't age. True, above on a face or two,
a wrinkle—though the dance is below: the leg show
    is friskier far.

And I—should a century join the dance—
we just sit here alone
(like spectators) clapping our hands
in the creaking armchair of our bones!

Execrable Cold

Windy, barbarously windier day by day,
the open country unprotected by hills:
suddenly disclaimed by the sky,
betrayed. Yesterday
the Sun still spilled off embers. At night
the stars were like sparks and ash dust. And today
that ancient principle of Naught, the cosmic freeze,
hurls to the earth the antilife.
Everything's more pathless
here in the land nourished by life.
The field and forest game
stealthily nose for territory
in the snow smelling of nothing.
And under its iron law, imposed
     by fate,
the human race will also be more warlike.
Opposed to what its future promises—
Year by year the winter is more barbarous.
     More futureless.

Man and Mob

Step-by-step I precede my events.
Step-by-step I pursue my events.
In their tracks, yet where to?
Namely, among them.
Forcing my feet
to be docile pressing the muscles
of my face into order distrustful
watchful that my voice box
not go baa.

Omnipotence

I, not know what omnipotence is?
     On my steed ancient
     as Rosinante,
on our draft nag in the muck at the village
    limits, I trotted with a schoolboy's
certitude and conceit. Modern world!
    —already, with the fevered heroics
    of class warfares, putting to flight
      the army of
      ducks and chicks.

I know what pride is,
    yours,
as you hunt even him who
    hides his sores.

1983

[My wife had two walls one brick thick]

My wife had two walls one brick thick built in the attic of the old family house, and though the frost bites in winter, and in the heat of summer even a shirt makes me sweat—here I have a private place, and time, and also a far-off view above Pest and the Danube; in fact even farther, with gentle ghostlike eyes to the Székely outposts.

Like the "suspended passageways" on apartment houses, a footwalk of fifteen paces runs in front of this refuge: the wide—let's call it a balcony—on which I walk up and down in the evening to take the air, an exiled chieftain.

. . . going to and fro with the preoccupations of tolerated jesters of yore, I air the worry, I air the worry—of how many days and how many millennia—that has devolved on me, unasked.

Generals, Victory

All the battlefields—Catalaunum, Verdun—
are a segment only of where body, body, body
lies fallen, scattered, heaped up endlessly
as far as the eye can reach, or imagination.
On the right—now silent—the counterarmy. There
on the left—equally silent—the attacker.
In the middle, the victor. You. I. The general: who
has survived. And lives today. Tomorrow too.

Elephant Cemetery

Here those gather together who stand by leaning
against each other, if they still can stand.
Such final conjoinings are legion, meaning
they're made by nation, people, animal, man
ready to die because they stand their ground.
The cemetery is not for the dead. Not yet:
they mark time, though their legs are giving out.
Is it soon that that Tomorrow will come round,
that glorious, that heroic End
the *vates* sang about!

Now and then a trunk shaped like a trombone
reaches upward to sound a proclamation,
but all that comes out is a sort of rasping sound
—verifying its isolation—
in a voice hoarse with tears and self-derision:
much like this poem—and how many others?—about
to be left unfinished since faith is running out.

You Urged Me On

You urged me on as
the bright mountain peaks above me.
You praised me as
the fertile parti-colored plains beneath me.

The mouth-curves of the river,
approving bashfully.

And you stood opposite
and handed over a child,
a key to shut the past,
a key to open the future.

Day by day you crowned me
more visibly than the dawn
as a born hero, and after
my army's daily rout
you rescued me into your island.

Not dream and oblivion:
you rescued me evening by evening.

1983

[How shall I end?]

How shall I end? I do not know. No matter . . .
I know the farewell word:
I order that you outlive me,
that each of your steps be blest,
that the sin you judge you live unconscious of—

February 21–25, 1983

■ □ ■ □ ■

WRITINGS FROM AN UNBOUND EUROPE

Tsing
Words Are Something Else
DAVID ALBAHARI

City of Ash
EUGENIJUS ALIŠANKA

Skinswaps
ANDREJ BLATNIK

My Family's Role in the World Revolution and Other Prose
BORA ĆOSIĆ

Peltse and Pentameron
VOLODYMYR DIBROVA

The Victory
HENRYK GRYNBERG

The Tango Player
CHRISTOPH HEIN

A Bohemian Youth
JOSEF HIRŠAL

Charon's Ferry
GYULA ILLYÉS

Mocking Desire
Northern Lights
DRAGO JANČAR

Balkan Blues: Writing out of Yugoslavia
JOANNA LABON, ED.

The Loss
VLADIMIR MAKANIN